# Mother, I Love You Forever

Other books by

# Blue Mountain Press INC

Books by Susan Polis Schutz:

**Come Into the Mountains, Dear Friend**
**I Want to Laugh, I Want to Cry**
**Someone Else to Love**
**Yours If You Ask**
**Love, Live and Share**
**Find Happiness in Everything You Do**
**Don't Be Afraid to Love**
**Take Charge of Your Body**
by Susan Polis Schutz and Katherine F. Carson, M.D.

**Warmed By Love**
by Leonard Nimoy

**I'm on the Way to a Brighter Day**
by Douglas Richards

Anthologies:

**Creeds to Love and Live By**
**With You There and Me Here**
**Reach Out for Your Dreams**
**I Promise You My Love**
**Thank You for Being My Parents**
**A Mother's Love**
**A Friend Forever**
**You Are Always My Friend**
**It Isn't Always Easy**
**My Sister, My Friend**
**Thoughts of Love**
**Thoughts of You, My Friend**
**You Mean So Much to Me**
**Love Isn't Always Easy**
**Don't Ever Give Up Your Dreams**
**When I Think About You, My Friend**
**I Love You, Dad**
**I Keep Falling in Love with You**
**I Will Always Remember You**
**For You, My Daughter**
**A Lasting Friendship**
**I Will Love You**
**Through Love's Difficult Times**
**Though We Are Apart, Love Unites Us**
**Always Follow Your Dreams**

# Mother, I Love You Forever

a collection of poems
Edited by Susan Polis Schutz

**Blue Mountain Press** ™

Boulder, Colorado

Library of Congress Number: 85-73819
ISBN: 0-88396-245-4

The following works have previously appeared in Blue Mountain Arts publications:

"To My Mother," by Susan Polis Schutz. Copyright © Stephen Schutz and Susan Polis Schutz, 1981. "To My Mother," by Susan Polis Schutz. Copyright © Stephen Schutz and Susan Polis Schutz, 1983. "My Ideal Mother," by Susan Polis Schutz. Copyright © Stephen Schutz and Susan Polis Schutz, 1984. "I want to thank you, Mother," by Barbara Lemke; and "Whenever I have a problem," by Sheilah D. Street. Copyright © Blue Mountain Arts, Inc., 1984. "You come to mind so often," by Lisa Ford; "Mother . . . I've always wanted," by Shirley Paceley; and "You were always there," by Lenore Turkeltaub. Copyright © Blue Mountain Arts, Inc., 1985. "I Love You Forever, Mother," by Susan Polis Schutz. Copyright © Stephen Schutz and Susan Polis Schutz, 1986. "In Your Footsteps, Mother," by Danine Winkler; "Dear Mother," by Deanna Beisser; "Mother, as you," by Ann Rudacille; "For all the times," by Bonnie Bachman Bragg; "Mother, you give me love," by Donna Levine; and "Your love for your mother," "I have always kept my feelings," "When someone cares," "For All the Times," "My Feelings for My Mother, " "A Family Is Love," and "People like you," by Collin McCarty. Copyright © Blue Mountain Arts, Inc., 1986. All rights reserved.

Thanks to the Blue Mountain Arts creative staff.

ACKNOWLEDGMENTS appear on page 62.

Manufactured in the United States of America
First printing: January, 1986

# Blue Mountain Press INC.

P.O. Box 4549, Boulder, Colorado 80306

# CONTENTS

## I Love You Forever, Mother

You have shown me how to give of myself
You have shown me leadership
You have taught me to be strong
You have taught me the importance of the family
You have demonstrated unconditional love
You have demonstrated a sensitivity
    to people's needs
You have handed down to me the important
    values in life
You have handed down to me the idea
    of achieving one's goals
You have set an example, throughout your life
of what a mother and woman should be like
    I am so proud of you
        and I love you
            forever

— Susan Polis Schutz

## For You, Mother

As my first friend,
you introduced me to a life enriched
by your love and warmth . . .
you shaped the way I feel about the world
and my place in it today.

Your confidence in me
helped me to believe in myself,
and your praise and respect
enabled me to appreciate my own worth.

You guided without control
and encouraged without pressure.
You gave your best . . .
to bring out the best in me.

You taught me to think my own thoughts
and to follow my own dreams;
to be proud of my achievements
and accepting of my mistakes;
to find peace in each sunset
and joy in each sunrise . . .
to love my life.

You knew what to say
and how to listen
to help me through the rough times
and to make the good times
even more beautiful.
I took it for granted
that you'd be there when I needed you
. . . and you always were.

As I grew older,
I made many new friends,
but of all the kindness they have shown me,
your understanding is still the deepest,
your companionship the warmest,
and your support the most generous.

I thank you, Mother,
for all you have been to me —
my first friend . . .
    and my best friend.

— Paula Finn

## To My Mother — I Love You

You come to mind so often . . .
and I wonder why I have been chosen
to have a wonderful, loving
    parent like you.

You have given me love . . .
    welcoming me home with open arms.
You have given me courage . . .
    helping me in times of need.
You have given me security . . .
    knowing I have a safe home and
    a special family to return to always.
You have given me trust . . .
    from always being able to
    believe in me, and I in you.
You have given me honesty . . .
    knowing that we always speak
    the truth with each other.
And you have given me friendship . . .
    helping me to realize that I am
        never alone; you are always near.
I want so much to repay you
for your kindness,
and someday I will find a way . . .
but for now I can only tell you,
    though I don't always show it
        and though I don't always say it . . .
        I love you.

— Lisa Ford

## In Your Footsteps, Mother

Mother, my words of love to you are
not just for any special occasion, but
because there is a very special bond
between mother and child.
I remember so long ago when I
followed so closely behind you . . .
you protected my every move
while holding my hand, and
your love never failed me.
As I've grown from year to year,
your hand opened to allow my
reaching out and growth.
You watched me strive and achieve,
with so much pride and silent prayer.
You also let me fail on my own,
but were always there to pick me up
while we shared the tears.

Maybe words can never fulfill
just how much is in my heart, but
I want you to know that I've learned
so much from you, and silently

I will always reflect, with smiles
    and grateful tears,
upon our moments together.
I've realized that I may no longer
follow behind you as I did when I
was small; instead, our footsteps
have become equal strides as we
walk side by side, together in friendship.
Mother, I don't know if I can ever
repay you for the gifts of life.
But if I can live my life by giving
to others as much as you have
    given to me . . .
I will be following in your footsteps
    once again.

— Danine Winkler

Dear Mother,
I know it's not your birthday
or your anniversary
or even Mother's Day.
It's just an ordinary day.
I don't need any money,
and I don't have a problem
to solve . . .
I just wanted
to say,
"I love you."

— Deanna Beisser

## Whenever I'm
## Away from Home, Mother

Your love for your mother
is something that you
never completely comprehend
until you are
    separated by the miles
from her warmth
    and her wonder.

When I was living at home,
I took so many things
    for granted
    without ever meaning to.
And I always knew
what a precious person you were,
but I never really took the time
to go beyond the thought . . .
    and into what you really
        meant to me.

Now that I'm without you
by my side, I find myself
thinking of you so often . . .
hoping in a way that it will
bring you a little closer to me.

And in those thoughts
I always come to the conclusion
that you are more than my mother;
you're a counselor and a companion;
you're a dear friend and a happy home;
you're a thousand beautiful memories;
    and you're someone whom I love
        with all my heart.

— Collin McCarty

Mother,
as you well know,
I have become involved
   in too many things,
and I don't write to you
as often as I should.
Maybe you wonder, at times,
if I have forgotten you
and if I need you less than I used to,
and I can understand
how I might cause you to feel that way.
It's true that I am very busy
much of the time,
but I never get too busy to tell
my friends what a wonderful mother
I have,
and that without you,
I would have nothing,
because you are everything to me.
   And no matter how full my life gets,
      it could never be as full
         as my heart is —
            with love for you.

— Ann Rudacille

Mother . . . I've always
    wanted you to know
my special feelings for you.

Growing up was hard for me.
I know I was a difficult child,
but what got me through
    and what made me okay
was knowing you were
    always there.

I'll never forget
    the caring in your eyes.
You let me grow and
    allowed me to explore.
I love you for
    letting me be me.

Your life touches mine
            every day . . .
in the way I look,
    the words I speak . . .
they have all come from you
            in some special way.

I am so
    thankful for you, Mother.

You are the gift
    that I was born with.

                    — Shirley Paceley

## For You, Mother

I want to thank you, Mother,
because a long time ago, you gave me
the most precious gift I'll ever
    receive — my life.
It's a gift I can share with others,
a gift that grows in value over time.
Thank you for enabling me to receive
    all the love showered upon me,
not only today, but every day;
for enabling me to experience all
    that life has to offer . . .
your love, my time, life's beauty.
You have given me the most promising,
    useful gift,
the gift I celebrate today and every day.
    Mother . . .
            thank you for me.

— Barbara Lemke

For Mother, with all my heart

I have always kept
my feelings for you
   in the most precious place
         within me.

There is a place in my heart
that learned,
   from the very beginning,
         what love was all about.
Whether you know it or not,
   you taught me a beautiful lesson about life:
      that giving is receiving, and that the circle
      of love is never as complete
         as it is in a family like ours.

My memories of home
   go with me wherever I go,
      and they keep me close to you . . .

I know that I
   will never stop thanking you
      for everything you are to me
         and for everything you do.

— Collin McCarty

For a Special Person in My Life —
My Mother

I can't imagine my life
without your loving presence . . .

When I look back on my important "firsts,"
I remember how you shared in my excitement.
When I recall sadder occasions,
I see the concern in your eyes
and the comfort in your smile.
When I think of times
when I was afraid to move forward . . .
I hear your gentle words of encouragement.

You eased me through many of my growing
    pains
with your humor and your patience.
You helped me to get in touch
with who I was . . .
and encouraged me to be better.
You believed in my dreams
and gave me the confidence to follow them.

You taught me to find hope in disappointment
and success in failure . . .
to be happy with the world,
and more important,
to be happy with myself.

You always had time for me,
whether to advise
or simply to listen . . .
Your understanding
made my problems seem lighter,
my hopes stronger,
and my joys deeper.

You set an example
of kindness and compassion,
and I hope I have incorporated
at least some of your strengths
into my own life.

You're a very special person to me,
and although my words don't often tell you,
I hope that somehow my actions
communicate how much
I admire and respect you . . .
    and how deeply I love you.

— Paula Finn

## To My Mother

For as long as I can remember
you were always by my side
to give me support
to give me confidence
to give me help

For as long as I can remember
you were always the person
    I looked up to
so strong
so sensitive
so pretty

For as long as I can remember
and still today
you are everything
a mother should be

For as long as I can remember
you always provided stability
    within our family
full of laughter
full of tears
full of love

Whatever I have become
is because of you
and I thank you
forever
for our
relationship

— Susan Polis Schutz

I know, Mother, that I've never truly
   communicated to you
   how much I love you . . .
I have always tried to show you
   in my actions,
but seldom have I tried to put
   my feelings into words.
I realize at times I've disappointed
   you,
but when I did, you never acted
   disappointed,
      only gentle and understanding.
I've always sensed, Mother,
   that you'd give just about
      anything to make me happy . . .
but more importantly,
you showed me that I can do that
   for myself.
Your love has taught me so much,
   and I want to take this time
      to put my feelings into words . . .
            I love you.

— Janice Lamb-Giuglianotti

## To You, My Mother

The memories are still there —
the time I bumped my knee,
and you came running
to bandage my heart
and wipe my salty tears . . .
the time I failed my test,
and you told me
it wasn't the end of the world,
that I would do better next time . . .
the time I made the wrong decision,
and you gave me the freedom
to learn from my mistake,
never holding it against me . . .
Yes, the memories are still there —
memories of an exceptional parent
always understanding, always loving,
    always caring,
and always there when I needed you
    most.

— Jeri Sweany

## To Mother, with Love

You were always there
    whenever I needed you.
Caringly, patiently, and lovingly,
    you showed me right from wrong.
You helped me to develop values
    that became the solid foundation
    upon which I continue to build.

Not only did you offer encouragement,
but you also cheered and praised me
    on to success.

Because you made me feel
    special and important,
I have been able to regard myself
    with respect and know
that I am a worthwhile individual.

Many passing seasons have caused me
    to see and understand more clearly,
and to more fully appreciate
    the constancy of your guidance.

Thank you, Mother, for giving me
    a priceless heirloom — your love.

— Lenore Turkeltaub

## Mother

Whenever I have a problem, it
    becomes our problem.
You support me in whatever decisions
    I make,
and even when I'm wrong, you stand
    beside me
because you realize that's when I
    need you the most.
Your belief in me is so strong
that you've made me believe in
    myself.
Even though I am no longer a child,
you are still helping me to grow.
I can always depend on you,
not just because you're my parent,
but because you're also my friend.

— Sheilah D. Street

Mother, you'll always be in my heart . . .

**W**hen someone cares about their family
as much as I care about mine,
that caring is the result of so many things . . .
   of thousands of precious memories,
   of love given from the heart,
   of being like best friends to each other.

It's a love that is nurtured from
lives that will always be intertwined . . .
   through all joy and every sorrow,
   beyond today, in each tomorrow,
      always cheering each other on,
         always helping and hoping for the best.

I don't know if other people feel
as strongly about their family
   as I care about ours — I just remember
loving everything about it
   from the very start. And that love
      is something I will keep
         and cherish forever . . .
in the home that will always be
         in my heart.

— Collin McCarty

## My Ideal Mother

An ideal mother should be
strong and guiding
understanding and giving
An ideal mother should be
honest and forthright
confident and able
An ideal mother should be
relaxed and soft
flexible and tolerant
But most of all
an ideal mother should be a
loving woman
who is always there when needed
and who
by being happy and satisfied
with herself
is able to be happy and loving
with her children
Mother, you are a rare woman —
you are everything an
ideal mother should be

— Susan Polis Schutz

With you as my mother . . .

**P**lease . . . bear with me
as I plan my life.
Sometimes I'm impatient, and
I feel like I'm wasting time.
I get depressed and feel like
I'm not moving anywhere.
I feel like a failure sometimes,
but I know I'm not.
How could I be . . . with
you for a parent?

Just remember sometimes
when I complain or don't help out
as much as I should,
that my mind is elsewhere,
dreaming in the future
and thinking about my feelings.

So bear with me. I know it's hard.
I know I can be difficult.
But I'm a dreamer . . .

Sometimes I just need to be alone
and think.
Thank you for raising me
to aspire, to yearn for more,
to hope, to strive.
I sure am going to try . . .
even though it can be
a scary world out there.
But I know that somehow
everything is all right.
Whenever I turn out the light
at bedtime,
I feel the love that you hold
and I know that you care.

Inside I know
that everything's all right . . .
because I've got you
for a parent.

— Sharon Johnson

For you, Mother

Ever since
I've been old enough
    to remember,
you have been there
whenever I needed you . . .
    to share my troubles
    to laugh with me
        when I was happy
    to love me most
        when I was hurt.
So many memories . . .
memories I hold most dear,
and that will be cherished forever.
For not only have you been
    my mother
    and my best friend,
    but also the woman
    I most want to be like
        in life.

— Debbie Avery

## Mother, You Taught Me Love

From no one else have I learned
as much about love
as from you, Mother.

The sacrifice in your love taught me
love is only love when it is unselfish;
love is only love when given freely
and unconditionally.

The forgiving nature of your love
showed me love forgives completely
and renews itself.

The honesty in your love taught me
to say, "I'm sorry," and showed me
the power of those two words
to hold love together.

Above all, you have taught me
  that happiness is there
    for those who live love.

I realize now that I have only
  been able to give more love to others
    because I have been given more love
      than others.

And for this, and everything else . . .
  I love you, Mother.

— Darryl Wilbur

## For All the Times, Mother

For all the times I turn to you
and you are always there,
     I thank you dearly.

For all the times when you are
my sun smiling through in
a cloudy sky,
     I thank you warmly.

For all the times you tell me
that tomorrow will be better,
I thank you for helping me
to make it so.

For all the times I count on you,
I thank you with all my heart
for never letting me down.

For all you do, and
for all you have done,
I thank you with everything within me.
And I want you to know,
even if I don't always say so,
that appreciating you
     is something I have always done
     and something I will
          always do.

— Collin McCarty

## Thanks, Mother

**S**ometimes, it seems that only after
we move away from home do we realize
what we truly had. Miles away, I
miss you, and I rely on the advice
you gave me while I was growing.
It's like having you by my side.
All I have to do is think, "What
would Mother suggest?" and
the answer is clear.

Thank you for caring and for
being wise. The knowledge I've gained
is a part of you I carry within me
wherever I go.

— Barb Harwood

## My Feelings for My Mother

Whenever I get lonely,
all I have to do is
imagine myself home with you.

You're the person
who means the most to me
in my life,
and it sometimes makes me
sad to think that we don't
see each other more often
than we do.

But though we're not together
as often as I'd like us to be,
we are — and always will be —
together in so many
wonderful family feelings.
The most special place
in my heart
will always be saved
for you.

— Collin McCarty

Mother . . . A Family Is Love

Wherever we go,
   and whatever we do,
let us live with this
remembrance in our hearts . . .
   that we are family.

What we give to one another
comes full circle.
May we always be
   the best of friends;

may we always be one another's
rainbow on a cloudy day;
as we have been yesterday
and today to each other,
may we be so blessed
in all our tomorrows . . .
over and over again.

For we are a family,
and that means love
that has no end.

— Collin McCarty

I will always love you, Mother

**S**o much of yourself and your love
you've given me.
You've taught me to care about myself,
about others,
and how to give love,
because only in giving do we receive,
and love is what life is all about.
You've shared your interests,
your dreams,
your beliefs,
and helped me to discover
what I can do,
and who I can be.
With everything that keeps you busy
you've always seemed to find the time
to share a moment,
a laugh, a tear
when it most counts.

You've taught me to understand
what I feel inside . . .
that it's okay to be angry
or scared,
happy or sad.
Somehow you always knew,
even when I couldn't see it,
that tomorrow would be
another day, a brand-new day
with new dreams,
to be whatever I make it to be.

For all you've given me —
especially for the gift of life —
I will always love you.

— Janis Knight

## Mother, the World Needs More People like You

People like you
are few and far between.
You are the special
   kind of person
      the world needs more of . . .

People like you
make everything so much nicer;
you have a marvelous ability
to turn happiness into joy
and sadness into understanding.

You are loved . . .
         for so many reasons,
and appreciated beyond words,
because people like you
   mean the world to . . .
         people like me.

— Collin McCarty

Mother, how I love you . . .

Time has passed
and I have grown; but still
I spend so much time
thinking of you and home
and how I love you . . .

For all the years
   you spent raising me;
For giving me love and food
   and shelter;
For all the times you helped me
   with my schoolwork, so that
   I might learn;
For all the times you protected me;
For a loving family and a strong
   family relationship;

For all the strength you passed along
    during times of pain and loss;
For all the sacrifices you
    made for me;
For all the times when I was down
    and you made me smile;
For accepting and welcoming
    my friends and making them
    feel at home;
For giving me moral support
    and confidence in the things
    I undertake;
For so many different things . . .
    I feel such love.

For loving me . . .
                        I love you.

— Jane Alice Fox

## To My Mother

When you have a mother
who cares so much for you
that anything you want
comes before her desires
When you have a mother
who is so understanding that
no matter what is bothering you
she can make you smile
When you have a mother
who is so strong that
no matter what obstacles she faces
she is always confident in front of you
When you have a mother
who actively pursues her goals in life
but includes you in all her goals
you are very lucky indeed
Having a mother like this
makes it easy to grow up
into a loving, strong adult
Thank you for
being this kind
of wonderful
mother

— Susan Polis Schutz

Dear Mother,
I sometimes feel the urgent need
  to thank you . . .
for all that you are,
for all that you've done.
For rooting my beginnings in the
rich soil of your nurturing, and
for treasured childhood memories.
For firm yet gentle hands that
set me free to try my wings . . .
enabling me to soar and grow.
For unconditional love.
How I've tested it through the years!
For always understanding that
growing up is never easy.
For patience, encouragement,
support, and sacrifice . . .
all the intangible, priceless
investments you've made in me.
For being you . . .
for making me possible.
I am eternally
your grateful child.

— Barbara Booth Gille

Mother, you're held close in my heart

There are few doors in my life that
I can enter without first knocking —
carrying no gift, no invitation, just
myself — and feel the immediacy of a
genuine welcome. Home has always been
one.

There are few people in my life who
have seen me at my very worst and my
very best — who I can be with or away
from, yet have no fear of being hastily
judged or unfairly criticized. You
have always been one.

There are few times in my life when
I have told you what you mean to me,
though I often believe you already
know. But I want this to be one of
those times . . .

For all the comforts of home,
the generous constancy of your love,
you are held warmly in my
thoughts, close in my heart,
and always with love and affection.

— Carol Ann Oberg

No one but you, Mother . . .

No one could ever make me laugh
as easily as you,
or restore my perspective so quickly
when the sun has disappeared
   from my day . . .

No one could understand me
as deeply as you,
by interpreting my words as I mean them,
sensing my unspoken thoughts,
and sharing my most private emotions . . .

No one could make me feel
as special as you,
by taking genuine interest
in what I think, say, and feel;
by always being ready
to give me the time I need,
and to appreciate the time I give . . .

No one could support me
as completely as you,
by sharing my sorrows as readily
    as my joys;
by accepting what I am —
and loving me for it.

No one could be better to me
than you . . .
and no one could appreciate you
    more than I do.

— Paula Finn

Thank you, Mother . . .

For all the times
I should have said it,
but didn't . . .
    Thanks!
For all the times
you deserved to hear it,
but didn't . . .
    I appreciate you so much!
And for all the emotion
I feel, but don't always
show it . . .
    I love you!

— Bonnie Bachman Bragg

For all that you are, Mother

Mother, you give me love.
You give me gentle encouragement
and tender affection.
I cherish our times together
because you are a sincere friend —
someone I can openly laugh with,
someone I can share a secret with,
someone I can trust and admire.
Our stormy times become fewer
as I grow to realize that our
disagreements are not as important
as the things we stand together on,
and there is never an argument
so important between us to make me
hold back my love from you.

I appreciate and love you, Mother,
for all that you are
and for all that you do.

— Donna Levine

# ACKNOWLEDGMENTS

We gratefully acknowledge the permission granted by the following authors to reprint their works.

Paula Finn for "For You, Mother," "For a Special Person in My Life," and "No one could ever." Copyright © Paula Finn, 1986. All rights reserved. Reprinted by permission.

Janice Lamb-Giuglianotti for "I know, Mother." Copyright © Janice Lamb-Giuglianotti, 1986. All rights reserved. Reprinted by permission.

Jeri Sweany for "To You, My Mother." Copyright © Jeri Sweany, 1986. All rights reserved. Reprinted by permission.

Sharon Johnson for "With you as my mother . . . " Copyright © Sharon Johnson, 1986. All rights reserved. Reprinted by permission.

Debbie Avery for "For you, Mother." Copyright © Debbie Avery, 1981. All rights reserved. Reprinted by permission.

Darryl Wilbur for "Mother, You Taught Me Love." Copyright © Darryl Wilbur, 1986. All rights reserved. Reprinted by permission.

Barb Harwood for "Thanks, Mother." Copyright © Barb Harwood, 1986. All rights reserved. Reprinted by permission.

Janis Knight for "So much of yourself." Copyright © Janis Knight, 1985. All rights reserved. Reprinted by permission.

Jane Alice Fox for "Time has passed." Copyright © Jane Alice Fox, 1986. All rights reserved. Reprinted by permission.

Barbara Booth Gille for "Dear Mother." Copyright © Barbara Booth Gille, 1985. All rights reserved. Reprinted by permission.

Carol Ann Oberg for "There are few doors." Copyright © Carol Ann Oberg, 1986. All rights reserved. Reprinted by permission.

A careful effort has been made to trace the ownership of poems used in this anthology in order to obtain permission to reprint copyrighted materials and to give proper credit to the copyright owners.

If any error or omission has occurred, it is completely inadvertent, and we would like to make corrections in future editions provided that written notification is made to the publisher: BLUE MOUNTAIN PRESS, INC., P.O. Box 4549, Boulder, Colorado 80306.